Potato Pals **1**

# Activity Book

## PATRICK JACKSON • RIE KIMURA

OXFORD
UNIVERSITY PRESS

198 Madison Avenue
New York, NY 10016 USA

Great Clarendon Street, Oxford OX2 6DP UK

Oxford University Press is a department of the University of Oxford.
It furthers the University's objective of excellence in research, scholarship,
and education by publishing worldwide in

Oxford  New York

Auckland  Cape Town  Dar es Salaam  Hong Kong  Karachi
Kuala Lumpur  Madrid  Melbourne  Mexico City  Nairobi
New Delhi  Shanghai  Taipei  Toronto

With offices in

Argentina  Austria  Brazil  Chile  Czech Republic  France  Greece
Guatemala  Hungary  Italy  Japan  Poland  Portugal  Singapore
South Korea  Switzerland  Thailand  Turkey  Ukraine  Vietnam

OXFORD and OXFORD ENGLISH are registered trademarks of
Oxford University Press

© Oxford University Press 2005

ISBN: 978 0 19 439190 0

Editorial Manager: Nancy Leonhardt
Senior Editor: Paul Phillips
Editor: Joseph McGasko
Associate Editor: Jessica Gillman
Art Director: Lynn Luchetti
Design Project Manager: Maj-Britt Hagsted
Designer: Michael Steinhofer
Production Manager: Shanta Persaud
Production Controller: Eve Wong

Illustrations by Rie Kimura

Additional realia by Vilma Ortiz-Dillon and Michael Steinhofer

Printing (last digit): 20  19  18  17  16  15

Printed in China

This book is printed on paper from certified and well-managed sources.

# Remember to...

# Connect. Color.

# Match. Color.

In the morning,

**1.**

**a.**

I wash my face.

**2.**

**b.**

I comb my hair.

**3.**

**c.**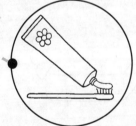

I brush my teeth.

**4.**

**d.**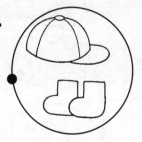

I get dressed.

# Trace. Match. Color.

**1.**

**a.**

soap

**b.**

flower

**2.**

**c.**

fork

**3.**

**d.**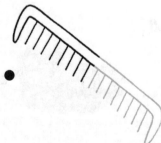

comb

**4.**

✓

# Circle. Color.

**1.** bed

**a.** 　　**b.** 　　**c.** 　　**d.**

**2.** glass

**a.** 　　**b.** 　　**c.** 　　**d.**

**3.** clock

**a.** 　　**b.** 　　**c.** 　　**d.**

**4.** towel

**a.** 　　**b.** 　　**c.** 　　**d.**

**5.** mirror

**a.** 　　**b.** 　　**c.** 　　**d.**

# Trace. Color.

# Find. Connect. Color.

red   yellow    pink 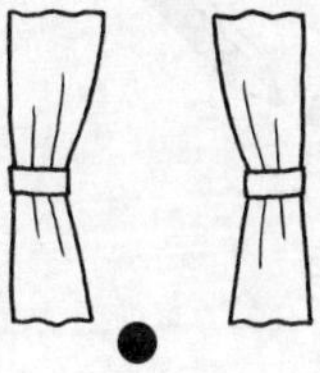   blue

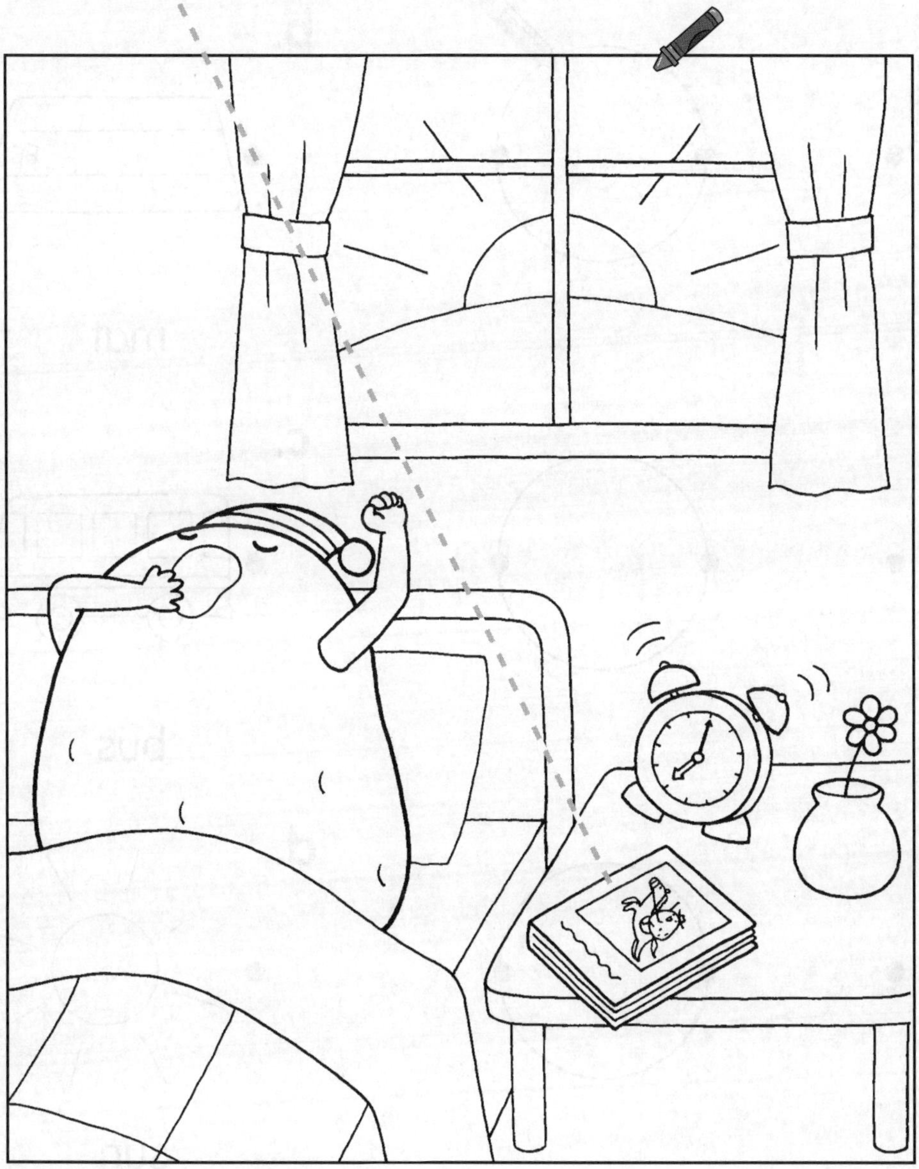

purple

green

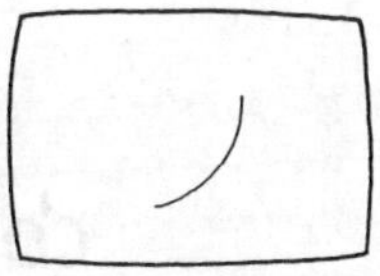

white

orange

## Connect. Write.

**1.**

mirror

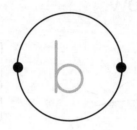
b

**a.**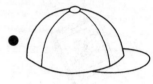

cap

**2.**

bed

s

**b.**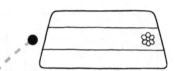

mat

**3.**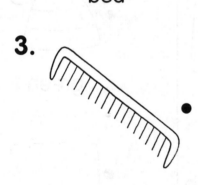

comb

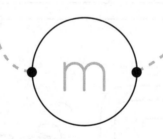
m

**c.**

bus

**4.**

soap

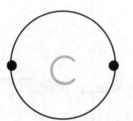
c

**d.**

sun

✓

8

# Connect. Color.

At school,

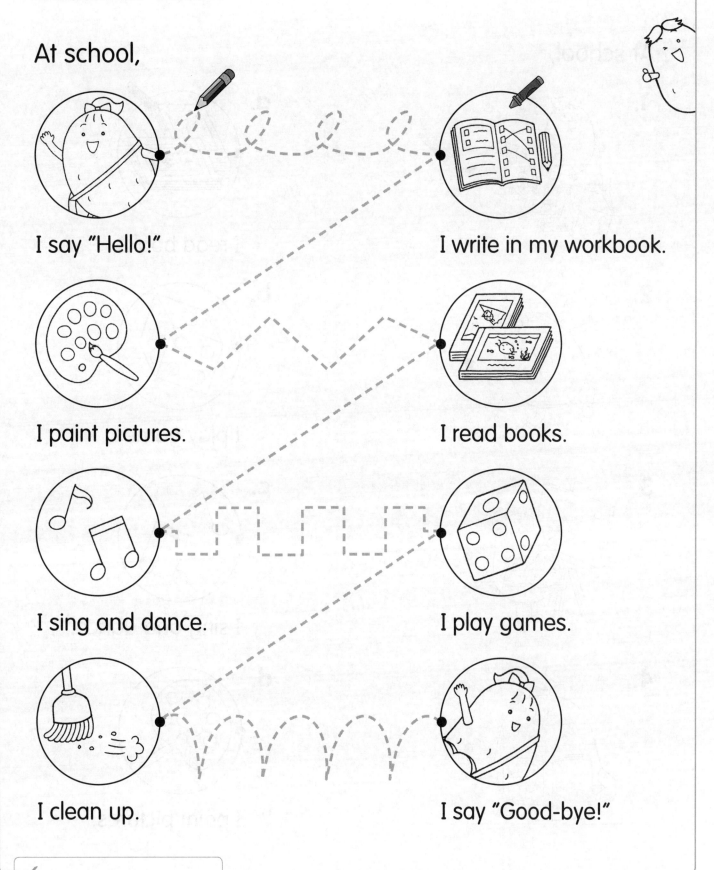

I say "Hello!"

I write in my workbook.

I paint pictures.

I read books.

I sing and dance.

I play games.

I clean up.

I say "Good-bye!"

## Match. Color.

At school,

**1.**

**a.**

I read books.

**2.**

**b.**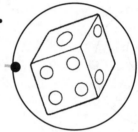

I play games.

**3.**

**c.**

I sing and dance.

**4.**

**d.**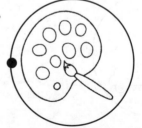

I paint pictures.

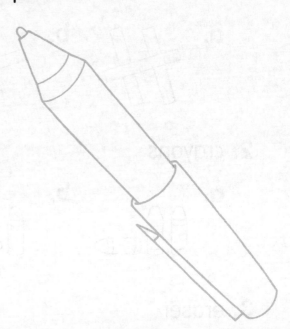

# Trace. Color.

**1.** scissors

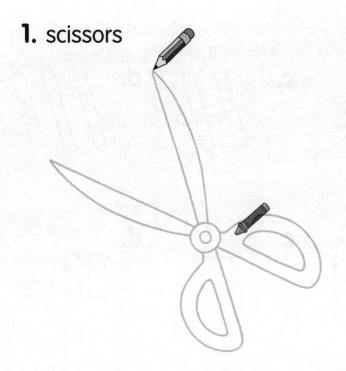

**2.** pen

**3.** globe

**4.** glue

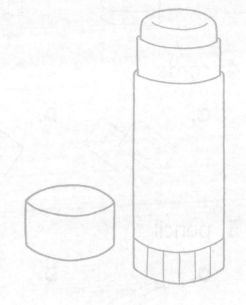

Nice work!

✓

# Circle. Connect.

**1.** ruler

**a.** 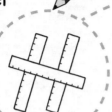    **b.**     **c.**     **d.**

**2.** crayons

**a.** 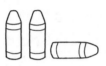    **b.**     **c.**     **d.**

**3.** eraser

**a.**     **b.** 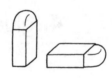    **c.**     **d.**

**4.** cards

**a.** 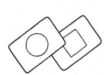    **b.** 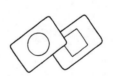    **c.** 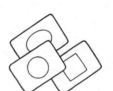    **d.**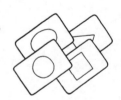

**5.** pencil

**a.**     **b.**     **c.**     **d.**

# Circle. Match. Color.

1.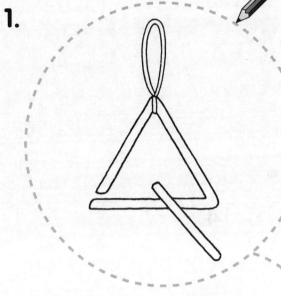

2.

3.

4.

a.

b.

c.

d.

Good job!

✓

13

# Trace. Match. Color.

**1.**

**2.**

**3.**

**4.**

**a.**

**b.**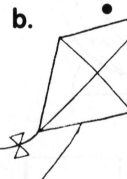

**c.**

**d.**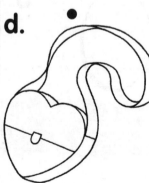

Great!

# Write. Connect. Circle.

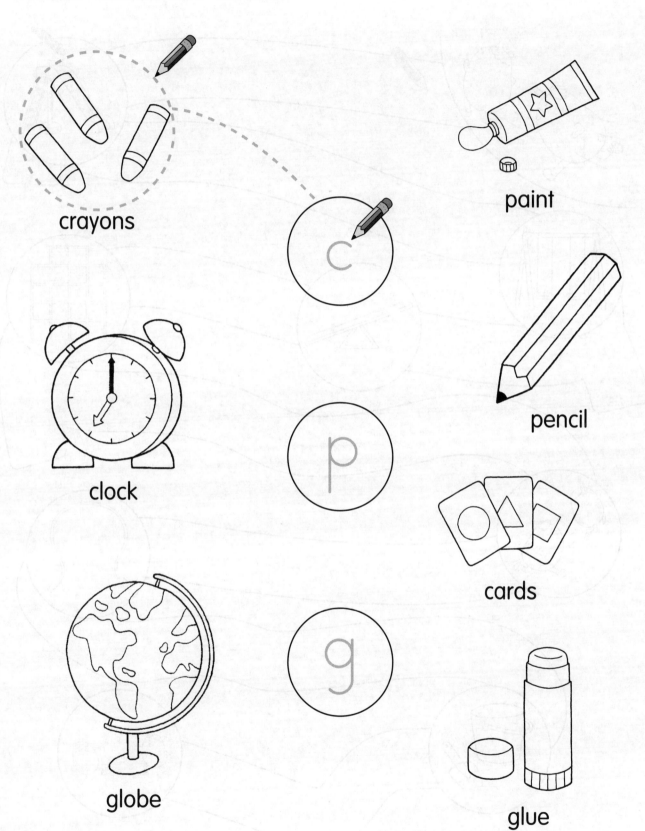

crayons

paint

c

clock

pencil

p

cards

globe

g

glue

# Connect. Color.

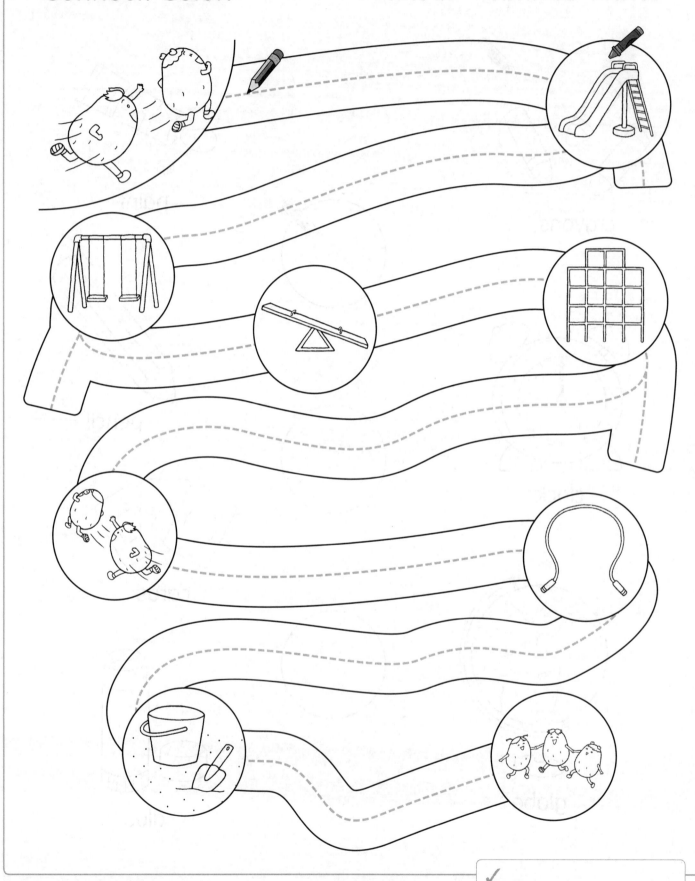

# Connect. Color.

At the park,

**1.**

**2.**

**3.**

**4.**

I slide on the slide.

I ride on the see-saw.

I swing on the swings.

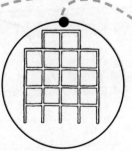

I climb on the jungle gym.

✓

# Trace. Draw. Color.

**1.** butterfly

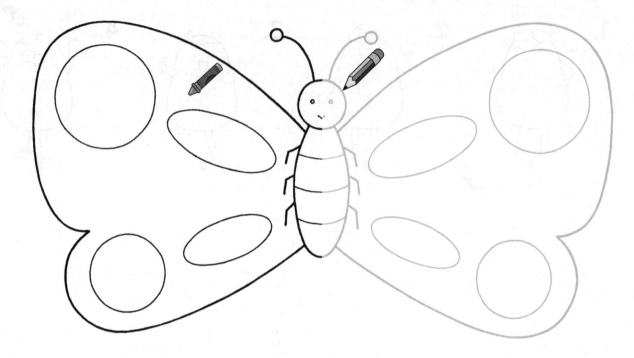

**2.** spider

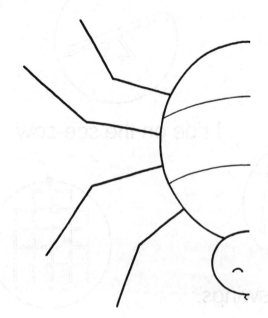

✓

**18**

# Match. Color.

**1.**

**a.**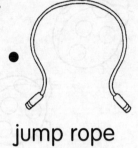

jump rope

**2.**

**b.**

bucket and shovel

**3.**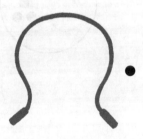

**c.**

tree

**4.**

**d.**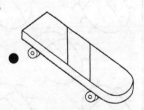

skateboard

Very good!

✓

# Match. Write. Color.

**1.**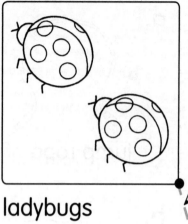

ladybugs

**2.**

grasshopper

**3.**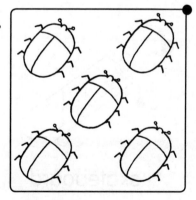

beetles

**4.**

birds

✓

20

# Circle. Write.

**1.** caterpillar 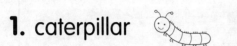 3

**2.** ant  4

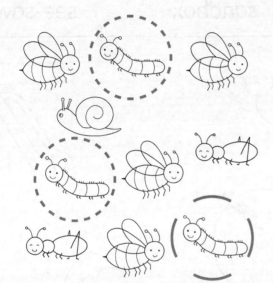

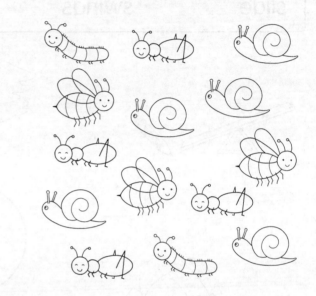

**3.** snail  6

**4.** bee  8

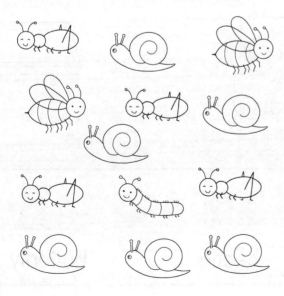

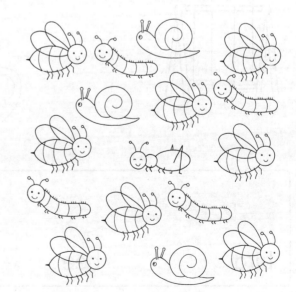

✓

# Write. Connect. Circle.

| | | | |
|---|---|---|---|
| slide | swings | sandbox | see-saw |

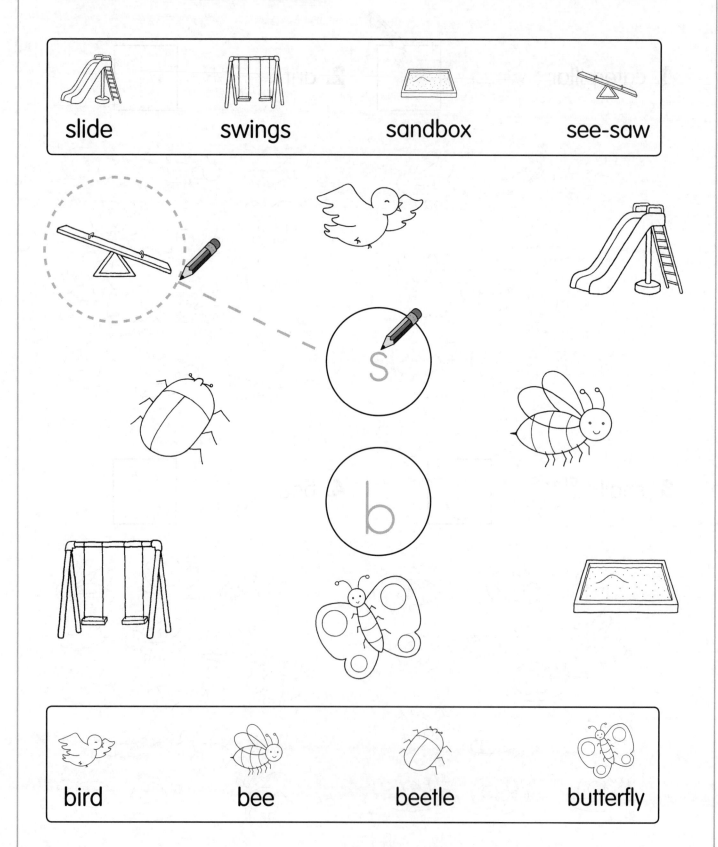

| | | | |
|---|---|---|---|
| bird | bee | beetle | butterfly |

# Trace. Connect. Color.

At home,

**1.** I make my bed.

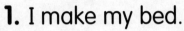

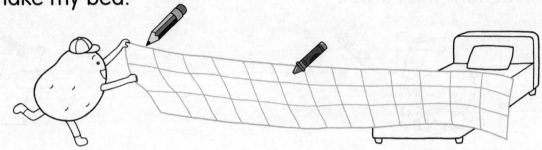

**2.** I take out the garbage.

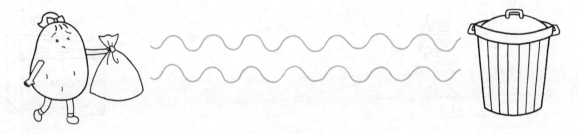

**3.** I do the laundry.

**4.** I take care of the baby.

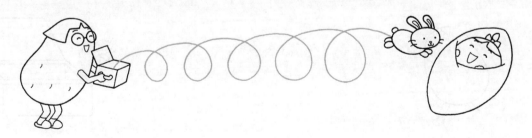

✓

# Trace. Connect. Color.

At home,

**1.** I vacuum the carpet.

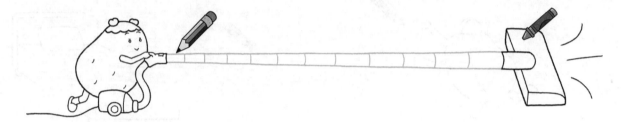

**2.** I clear the table.

**3.** I clean the bathroom.

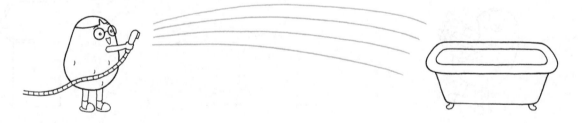

**4.** I put away my toys.

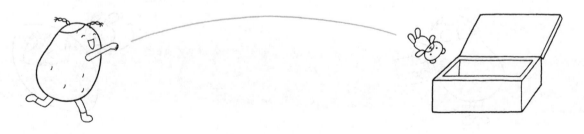

# Connect. Color.

**1.**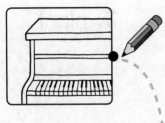

**a.** computer

**b.** piano

**2.**

**c.** washing machine

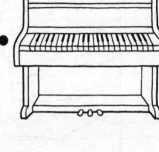

**3.**

**d.** garbage can

**4.**

**e.** vacuum cleaner

**5.**

Great!

# Find. Connect. Color.

**1.** cat

**2.** table

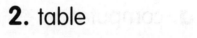

**3.** plant

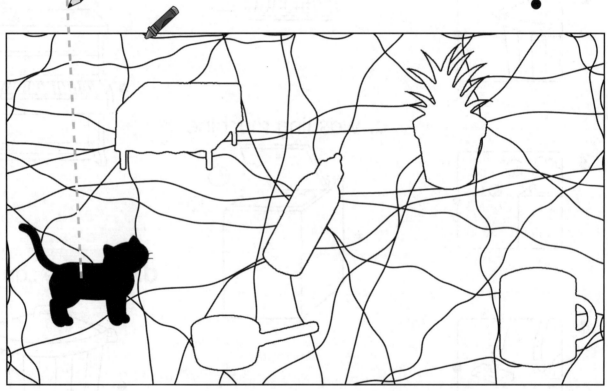

**4.**

baby bottle

**5.**

cup

**6.**

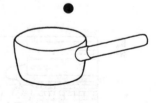

pot

✓

## Match. Color.

**1.** under the table

**2.** next to the cat

**3.** on the chair

**a.**

**b.**

**c.**

Very good!

# Find. Circle. Color.

# Write. Connect. Circle.

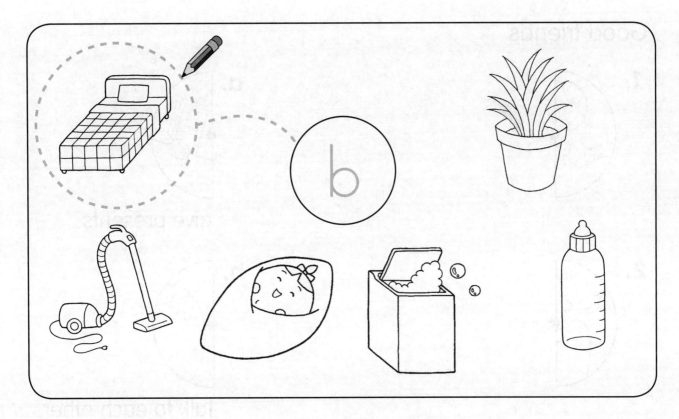

# Match.

Good friends

**1.**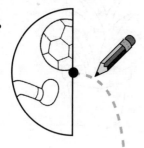

**a.**

give presents.

**2.**

**b.**

talk to each other.

**3.**

**c.**

share things.

**4.**

**d.**

play together.

# Match.

Good friends

**1.**   **2.**   **3.**   **4.**

**a.**

lend things.

**d.**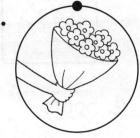

care.

**b.**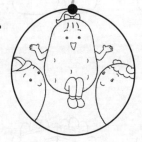

listen to each other.

**c.**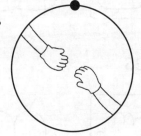

help each other.

✓

# Circle.

**1.** hat

**2.** scarf

**3.** umbrella

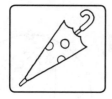    

**4.** boots

**5.** gloves

# Circle.

**1.** ball

**2.** lamp

**3.** ice skates

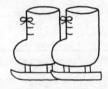    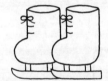  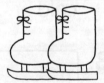

**4.** ice cream

**5.** present

✓

# Match.

**1.**
snowy

**a.**

**2.**
cold

**b.**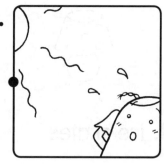

**3.**
cloudy

**c.**

**4.**
hot

**d.**

✓

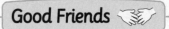

# Find the sunny day. Color.

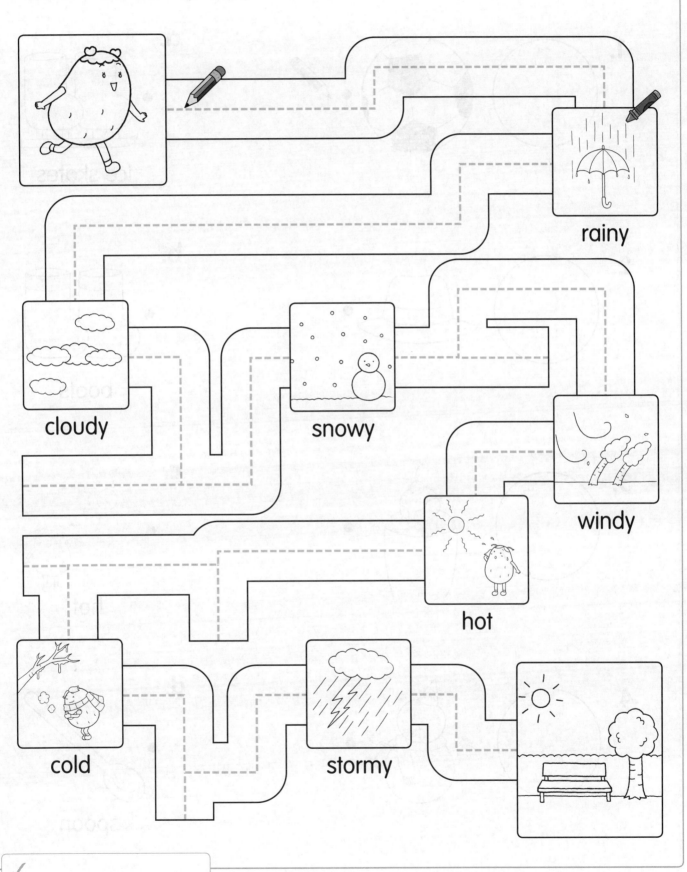

rainy

cloudy

snowy

windy

hot

cold

stormy

## Write. Connect.

**1.**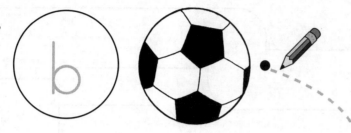

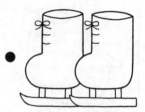

ice skates

**2.**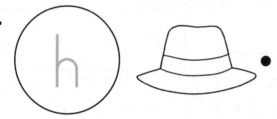

**b.**

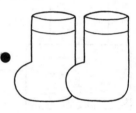

boots

**3.**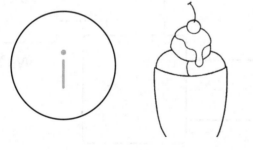

**c.**

hot

**4.**

**d.**

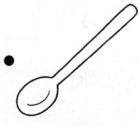

spoon

✓

# Match. Color.

In the evening,

**1.**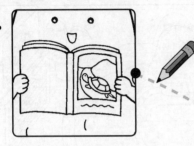

**a.**

I come home.

**2.**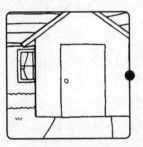

**b.**

I do my homework.

**3.**

**c.**

I read a story.

**4.**

**d.**

I go to sleep.

# Circle. Color.

**1.** I eat dinner.

a.

b.

**2.** I watch TV.

a.

b.

**3.** I take a bath.

a.

b.

**4.** I walk the dog.

a.

b.

## Connect. Color.

**1.**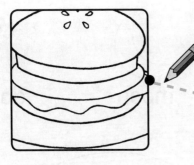

**a.**

TV

**2.**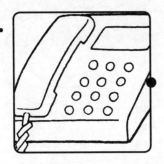

**b.**

hamburger

**3.**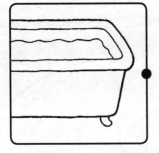

**c.**

telephone

**4.**

**d.**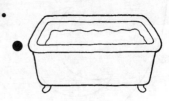

bathtub

# Find the missing item. Draw. Color.

 slippers

 newspaper

 bone

 moon

 dog

**1.**

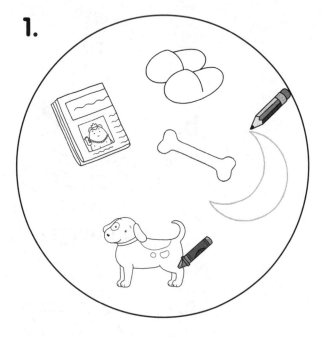

**2.**

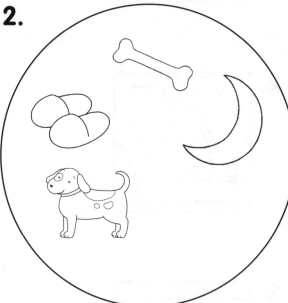

**3.**

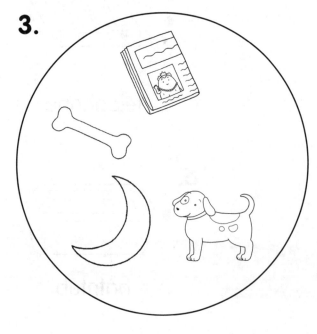

**4.**

# Circle. Connect. Color.

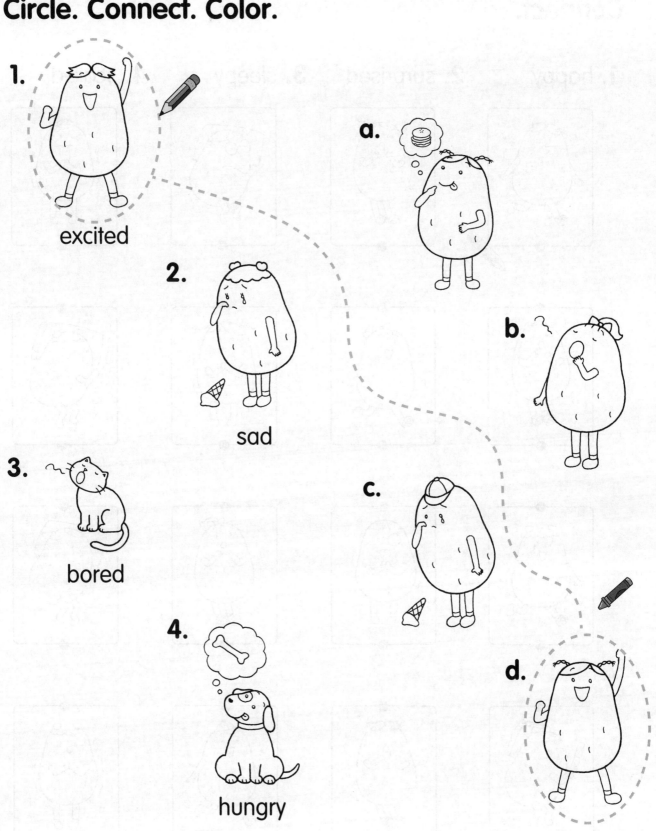

1. excited

2. sad

3. bored

4. hungry

a.

b.

c.

d.

# Connect.

**1.** happy     **2.** surprised     **3.** sleepy     **4.** scared

# Write. Connect. Circle.

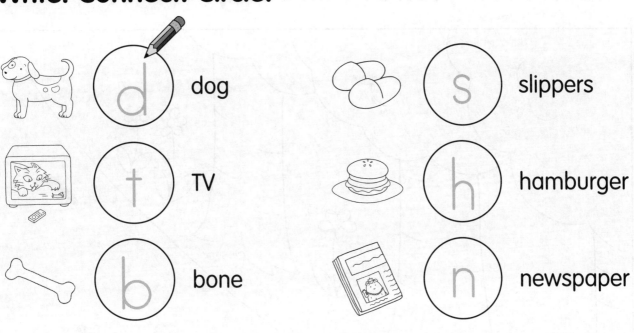

# Trace. Draw yourself with Buddy. Color.

# Trace. Draw yourself with Daisy. Color.

# Trace. Draw Joy's dinner. Color.